THE ART OF OVERCOMING FEAR

A Powerful Guide to Handle Fears, Build Personal Management Skills, Conquer Challenges, and Become Mega Successful in Life.

PRADIP DAS

© **Copyright 2024 - All rights reserved.**

The content contained within this book may not be reproduced, duplicated, or transmitted without direct written permission from the author or the publisher. Under no circumstances will any blame or legal responsibility be held against the publisher, or author, for any damages, reparation, or monetary loss due to the information contained within this book. Either directly or indirectly.

Legal Notice:
This book is copyright protected. This book is only for personal use. You cannot amend, distribute, sell, use, quote or paraphrase any part, or the content within this book, without the consent of the author or publisher.

Disclaimer Notice:
Please note the information contained within this document is for educational and entertainment purposes only. All effort has been executed to present accurate, up to date, and reliable, complete information. No warranties of any kind are declared or implied. Readers acknowledge that the author is not engaging in the rendering of legal, financial, medical or professional advice. The content within

this book has been derived from various sources. Please consult a licensed professional before attempting any techniques outlined in this book.

By reading this document, the reader agrees that under no circumstances is the author responsible for any losses, direct or indirect, which are incurred as a result of the use of information contained within this document, including, but not limited to, — errors, omissions, or inaccuracies.

Author Profile

Table of Contents

Table of Contents 4

Introduction 5

The Ills of Fear 9

The Best Way to Act Is Through Action 24

Be Comfortable with What You Know 28

Prioritize Values and Goals 32

Managing When You're Not in Control 35

Gaining Control 41

Taking Charge of Your Life 44

Planning for Success 52

Your Path to Success 56

Your Strategy for Success 61

Battling the Fear of Uncertainty 64

Conquer Your Fears 68

How To Overcome Fear 75

Conclusion 81

Introduction

A nation in crisis needs a strong leader. Someone who acts boldly, even when difficult situations. Franklin D. Roosevelt was such leader. His legs were weak, but his will was iron. As president, he faced down the Great Depression and World War II. Roosevelt proved that true courage isn't about being fearless. It's about doing what must be done, no matter how afraid you are.

Roosevelt didn't just talk. He acted. When banks were failing, he shut them down to stop panic. When people had no jobs, he created work programs. When Hitler threatened the world, Roosevelt led America into war.

He spoke directly to the people through radio "fireside chats." His words gave hope. His actions brought change. Even in a wheelchair, Roosevelt stood tall for America.

Other leaders can learn from this. Tough times will come. People will be scared. A real leader steps up then. They face problems head-on. They inspire others to be brave. Like Roosevelt, they show that a nation's strength comes from its spirit, not its fears.

Another remarkable example is Nelson Mandela, the anti-apartheid revolutionary who became the first black president of South Africa. Mandela spent 27 years in prison for his activism, enduring unimaginable hardship and isolation. Yet, he emerged from captivity with a spirit unbroken, leading his country through a peaceful transition to democracy and reconciliation.

Similarly, Winston Churchill, the Prime Minister of the United Kingdom during World War II, faced the fear of defeat and invasion from Nazi Germany. Despite overwhelming odds, Churchill rallied his nation with his stirring speeches and unwavering resolve, inspiring courage and resilience in the face of adversity.

You have goals and dreams, but the fear of what might happen if you fail is stopping you. This fear keeps many people from reaching their potential, leaving them stuck in a life where they never truly shine.

Fear, anxiety, and uncertainty are emotions we all face. Whether it's speaking up at work, worrying about job applications, or feeling anxious before a medical checkup, these feelings can be overwhelming. But there's hope. Instead of avoiding our fears, we can learn to face them head-on and find practical solutions that work in real-life situations.

This book is here to help you understand and conquer your fears. We'll discuss methods to manage anxiety and make better decisions. You'll learn how to identify your fears, understand what triggers them, and face them directly. Over time, with patience and persistence, you can change your relationship with fear and live a more fulfilling life.

Let's explore how to turn fear into courage, take control of our lives, and reach our true potential. This book will give you the tools and knowledge to break free from the chains of fear and achieve your goals. So, let's begin this transformation together.

The Ills of Fear

Fear is something we all experience in some capacity. Fear is there for a reason, as it can be a very effective motivator for specific situations.

But sometimes, our fears can get the best of us and consume us differently.

When this happens, it's known as having one or more Ills of Fear: a way to describe the different types of fears humans may experience.

- Fear of Nothing: This is when someone experiences an empty feeling in their mind, and they don't know what they're supposed to do next. This can be associated with numerous factors, from the lack of focus because we're all too distracted to the feeling that life is meaningless and there's nothing with any real value.

- Fear of Self: Similar to fear of nothing but applies specifically to how we view ourselves and our abilities and duties. This fear has existed since the beginning of time and is very easy to understand once you think about it. We are weak and vulnerable when born, so we need other people to help us get through life. But at some point, we grow up and start building our lives. We go to school or college to learn the skills and knowledge necessary for our future careers. We work to obtain the money that will allow us to live comfortably and do what we want while also giving us security in case anything wrong happens. We reach a certain age where we feel that our jobs are secure and nothing wrong can happen now because we have everything under control. But things slowly start to get complicated, and we realize that our jobs are not secure and that there are times when we have to work harder than before. Then, it's at this point where the fear of self comes into play, as we wonder if we will be able to handle these changes and if they will be too much for us.

- Fear of Loss: The fear of losing something or someone important to you. The fear of loss can come in different ways, such as losing something due to its destruction or losing someone due to them getting away from you.

- Fear of Abandonment: The fear of being left alone in your life. This usually happens when you feel you have no one to rely on, making you feel hopeless and sad.

- Fear of Change: This is when someone doesn't want to change their lives in any way, and they are unwilling to accept changes if they happen. Fearing change can be dangerous because we won't allow ourselves to experience new things that could improve our lives. It's perfectly normal not to want change, but what's important is knowing when it's needed and how we will deal with it once it happens.

- Fear of the Past: This fear keeps you from moving forward and living life to the fullest. It happens when you find yourself stuck in your past and feel that it's holding you back from achieving more in your life. This can also manifest in other ways, such as being stuck in a specific place or never leaving home because of traumatic experiences from our past.

- Fear of Insignificance: When we feel that we are not essential to anyone, which can make us feel sad about how our lives are right now. This fear can be very tough to tackle since it shows us how we are always so vulnerable and dependent on others, but there's a way to fix it. The most important thing to realize is that you're never alone and that other people also need you.

- Fear of Success: Similar to the previous fear, it's when someone feels that they can't handle fame and power. This happens when someone feels like they won't be able to control their success or the responsibilities that come with it. This is usually when fame and power go against their morals and what they feel is right in life, so they reject them altogether.

- Fear of Being Noticed: Fear of being noticed and stared at in public. This is hard to deal with because it doesn't make us feel good or comfortable when others constantly notice us. However, there's a way to get rid of it when you recognize how much others stare at you because they notice you're different instead of feeling threatened by them.

- Fear of Death: This is the fear that something will happen to us or those we care about in the future. The main thing you need to understand here is that nothing will happen in this case, and we need to stop worrying about it because there's nothing we can do about it anyway. It can be challenging when we think that the people we love might not be with us anymore, and it can make us lose hope if we don't prevent this from happening.

- Fear of Public Speaking: The fear of being in the spotlight and talking to many people at once. This can happen since we're a social species, so communication and talking to one another are crucial for our survival. However, some people sometimes like to avoid this as much as possible, and it's challenging to overcome this fear. This happens since when you're on stage or in front of an audience, you feel nervous since you know everyone is looking at you and evaluating you each second.

- Fear of Blood: Fear of blood. Usually, this fear is caused by intense scenes in movies and in real life. We all have feared that something terrible will happen to someone we care about because many things can happen when we see blood or when there's pointed attention on something that has it.

- Fear of Being Alone: When we feel like no one wants us around and no one wants to spend time with us. This happens because most people are very uncomfortable around vulnerable or weak people, and it's hard for them to accept you in their lives if you're vulnerable.

- Fear of the Unknown: The fear of things with unknown causes or effects. This is something we have to understand because it's very typical not to be sure about what will happen to us and what we're feeling right now is a part of that. It's not easy understanding everything that happens around us, but as we grow up, we start to figure it out, and our imagination isn't something scary anymore.

- Fear of Sleep: When someone fears sleep because they worry a lot about their dreams.

Since dreams are very personal and no two people dream the same thing, it makes us feel like there is some revelation waiting for us in our dreams.

- Fear of Starvation: The fear of death and wasting away. This usually happens to someone who has never been hungry in their life and had things given to them by others, and this can make us feel like someone is killing us slowly or want us to disappear.

- Fear of Winter: Fear of going outside in winter because you're afraid of the cold. Many people have a hard time dealing with being cold, and they don't like it, but once they realize much colder it is compared to summer, they will start developing a love for it since they'll be more comfortable.

- Fear of the Sea: The fear of being underwater or seeing the sea. This happens because we must understand that water is life, and it can be tough to understand how such a dangerous thing, like the sea, can be so crucial for our existence and lives. However, humans have an instinct to avoid what could be fatal for them, which makes us cautious at times.

- Fear of Abandonment: Fear of being alone. This is serious since it's related to the fear of being left behind by everyone and everyone you care about. This happens when you realize how much you love and need someone in your life, and the thought of being alone kills you.

- Fear of Hot Things: The fear of anything hot or warm. This usually happens because many people don't like the temperature too high, especially when there's no air conditioning on.

- Fear of Women: Fear of women because they represent something terrible that can happen to us. This mostly happens due to something in our past, but it can also happen when someone makes us uncomfortable when we interact with them.

- Fear of the Dark: Fear of the dark and things that go on in it. This happens because we know how important light is to see everything around us and how much we need it. After all, we need light to be able to recognize what's going on around us.

- Fear of Being Touched: Fear of being touched by other people, animals, or creatures. This can happen since we're comfortable interacting with other people, and it's only natural that when we try to touch another individual, they will feel uncomfortable since they have their boundaries and defend themselves from others.

How Fear Affects Success

Success isn't always easy to achieve, and sometimes it arrives without us understanding how we got there. True success requires more than persistence and hard work; it demands an understanding of our actions. Working hard without knowing if our efforts will pay off is unlikely to lead to the success we deserve.

People might say our dreams are unrealistic or impossible. However, we must recognize that while many things are beyond our control, opportunities often come from being in the right place at the right time or meeting someone who believes in us.

Our efforts can be futile without others' belief in us. Listening to our inner voice is crucial, and if we feel passionate about something, we should pursue it. Everyone has the power within themselves to succeed, and if they don't find success, they can still find happiness.

Fear is a strong emotion that makes us scared of potential outcomes. When it comes to success, fear can lead to failure by preventing us from trying new things. This fear makes us believe that everything will go wrong and that we'll never succeed unless we do what others tell us.

Fear can cause us to hold back or avoid new challenges because we're afraid of failing. It's important to understand that fear needs to be adaptable. Living in constant fear makes success difficult. Instead, we should learn from our mistakes and push through them.

For success, we must try new things and live with confidence. This might feel like going against the odds, but pushing forward with faith that everything will eventually work out is essential.

While there are many potential failures, listening to and trusting our inner voice helps us adapt and succeed. Experiencing ups and downs can make us fearful of the future, but these challenges are part of the process we must endure to achieve great success.

The fear of failure can be debilitating, but it doesn't have to defeat us. Some people settle for being average because they fear failure, but understanding the importance of what we do should motivate us to overcome fear.

Fear can keep us in our comfort zone, preventing us from living the life we deserve. If we give up when things get tough, fear will take over and drag us down, leaving no hope for progress.

Fear of failure affects success by holding us back from trying new things and making us doubt our abilities. However, if we don't let fear control our lives, we can achieve everything we want without anxiety.

Fear doesn't have to destroy us. By opening ourselves to new experiences and not letting fear dominate, we can create a fulfilling life. Fear is a part of life, but we must learn to manage it. Living in constant fear causes us to miss opportunities.

Overcoming fear is essential for success. Fear often makes us doubt ourselves and gives up too soon, but success is worth the effort. If something feels too difficult, seek help because people are always willing to lend a hand.

Fear is a significant obstacle to success, often preventing people from reaching their goals. If something in your life scares you, find a way to address it rather than avoiding it.

Making changes for success isn't easy and can be uncomfortable. However, we must face our fears and not let them control us. Trying new things is essential for reaching our full potential.

We shouldn't let our fears dictate our actions. Instead, we should face them and learn to live with them. Overcoming fear is challenging but necessary for achieving our goals.

Sometimes, people feel watched or judged when trying new things, but this discomfort is part of stepping out of our comfort zone. If you feel this way, remind yourself there's nothing to fear. Letting fear control us prevents us from growing.

Fear can hold us back from new opportunities and reaching our potential. We must not let it dictate our decisions or keep us from enjoying life. Some use fear as an excuse to avoid progress, but courage can help us overcome it.

Fear is simply an uncomfortable or nervous feeling. By overcoming it, we can gain valuable insights into life. Facing our fears enables us to live the life we deserve. If fear is holding you back, confront it and move past it to create a positive and fulfilling life.

The Best Way to Act Is Through Action

Fear is simply a lack of control over ourselves. If we can't control it, why fear it? Fearing only makes us more afraid over time. To overcome fear, we must understand what causes it.

Identify your fears and decide if they are real. If they aren't, don't let them bring you down. If they are, take action before they dominate your life. Many people have fears, but understanding them helps us prevent fear from controlling us.

Accept that you can't control everything, but that doesn't mean you'll be left behind. When something goes wrong, get up and try again instead of running away from fear. Face your fears head-on to overcome them. Let go of what's holding you back and be honest about your feelings.

Be confident in yourself and your emotions. Without this confidence, you'll always live in fear. No one can tell you exactly how to handle your fears because everyone's fears are different. The best way to overcome fear is to understand and confront it.

We all want to feel safe, but being afraid doesn't mean we have to let fear control us. If we don't deal with fear, it will grow until it takes over our lives. Fears often come from bad experiences, but they also teach us about ourselves. Don't let fear get you down; change how you feel about it.

Fear makes us feel helpless, but facing it head-on helps us regain control. If we don't address our fears, they will worsen. Taking action is the only way to overcome fear.

When faced with fear, don't let it control you. Understand it, and work through it. People often avoid facing their fears, but avoidance only makes things worse. I remember being afraid of the dark as a child, but facing it helped me overcome my fear.

Don't let fear stop you from living your life. Stand up for what you believe in and take action against your fears. If fear controls your life, do something about it. Otherwise, you're letting fear grow stronger.

The best way to deal with fear is to stop caring about what scares you. Fear makes everything seem more important than it is. If we don't control our fears, we can't live the life meant for us.

Even when something bad happens, fear eventually fades. Don't let fear control you; deal with it and understand what makes you afraid. Most people avoid their fears, but facing them head-on is the only way to overcome them.

Talking to someone who understands can help. Don't let your fears control you forever. I used to be scared of everything, but avoiding fear only made it worse. Believing in yourself is the key to overcoming fear.

Feeling scared is normal when facing new things. But if we know our fears will go away, we don't have to let them control us.

If you can imagine being afraid, try not to think about it. This helps prevent fear from controlling you.

Be Comfortable with What You Know

Be comfortable with what you know and how you feel because that is all you have.

Accept who you are and what you know because that's all you can do when dealing with life's challenges. Living in fear is never good, and if you're afraid of something new, you'll deal with that feeling until you get used to it or someone else overcomes it.

It's easier said than done because avoiding new experiences only makes us worse at handling anything outside our comfort zone. This approach won't bring happiness.

We can't let our fears control us. Constant worry is unhealthy, and if we give in to it, we'll end up doing nothing, no matter how much we want to act.

If you're scared of something, there may be no need to act on it immediately because most things will work themselves out in time.

Know how you feel and be okay with that feeling. Whatever makes you scared can only get better if you believe in yourself and try your best not to dwell on it. Without self-belief, fear won't go away, no matter how hard you try.

Allow yourself to get used to a situation before deciding it's too much. Many people find themselves in similar situations and try to make changes even when they're unsure if they're ready.

Fear often arises from the challenge of trusting others, particularly when we've experienced the loss of those who care about us.

If you're scared and avoid thinking about it, you'll only make yourself more nervous. There's always something that will come up that you'll have to deal with.

If we don't face our fears now, we'll never progress, regardless of our age. Fear can still hold us back.

Achieving anything will be challenging, but if you don't try your best, you won't succeed. Avoiding something out of fear only makes you more nervous because that fear will resurface.

We can't predict if something will go wrong, but you have to start believing in yourself. You never know what you're capable of until you try.

If you fail at something, move on. There's no point in being afraid of getting hurt or making mistakes. Just do what you want and stop being afraid of trying.

If we don't try, we'll never know what's out there for us. Thinking about how great something could be is pointless if we don't take steps toward it.

To stop feeling scared, you need to believe in yourself. When you're confident, you won't fear doing things outside your comfort zone. Trust your instincts; they'll guide you. If you're not confident, you won't accomplish anything.

Fears aren't real; they'll fade over time. Facing fears, even if it takes time, helps overcome them. Don't try to avoid fears; it'll only make them worse. Accept them and move forward.

Don't fear trying new things; it's how we learn. Don't worry about impressing others or being perfect; just be yourself. Don't stress over small things; they won't matter later on.

Being yourself means being comfortable with who you are. It makes others comfortable around you and develops better relationships. Don't worry about others' opinions; focus on your happiness.

Accept mistakes; they help us learn and improve. Don't fear judgment; instead, try new things together. Feeling good about yourself means not caring about others' opinions.

Prioritize Values and Goals

In life, it's essential to prioritize what truly matters and set goals that align with our values. By conquering fear and embracing our true selves, we can unlock our full potential and live a life of purpose and fulfillment.

Being disciplined means prioritizing what truly matters and setting realistic goals to overcome fear. Goals are effective when they're meaningful and achievable. Want to feel comfortable in your own skin? Trust your instincts and don't let others dictate how you feel about yourself. Our aim should be to empower those around us by accepting ourselves and learning from our mistakes. Achieving our goals requires effort and determination. We must witness progress firsthand to ensure success. Trying new things is essential for personal growth. If you're not open to new experiences, you're holding yourself back. Goals demand hard work and dedication. Without commitment, our efforts are in vain. Discovering our goals and understanding their significance in our lives is crucial for success. Recognizing when opportunities align with our goals is key to turning dreams into reality. Ruminating on thoughts or opinions won't lead to progress. Action is what drives change. Avoid unnecessary conflict. Fighting others only leads to internal strife and wasted energy. Focus on personal growth rather than trying to please everyone else. Authenticity frees us from the need for external validation. Stay true to yourself and pursue your goals relentlessly. Living in fear is limiting. Take risks and seize opportunities to live life to the fullest. Express yourself openly and honestly. Words have power, and sharing your thoughts can lead to positive change. Being disciplined means taking control of your own life and prioritizing your values and goals. Overcoming fear requires self-awareness and courage. Don't let fear hold you back from living your best life. Reflect on your choices and ensure they align with your values and goals. Don't let others dictate your path. Define your own journey and strive to live up to your potential. Conquer fear by taking action and living life on your own terms. Don't let fear dictate your life. Seize the moment and avail the opportunities that come your way.

Life is too short to live in fear. By prioritizing your values and goals, you can overcome obstacles and achieve greatness. So don't let fear hold you back—enjoy the journey and live life to the fullest!

Managing When You're Not in Control

Life can feel chaotic, leaving us feeling powerless. From job loss to constant change, maintaining a positive outlook can be tough. This chapter offers strategies for handling situations beyond your control, teaching patience and understanding until you can take action.

Many fear the unknown, like death or loss. Moments of indecision can leave us feeling powerless. But accepting uncertainty and being proactive can help us feel more in control.

To gain control, start by being honest with yourself. Analyze your feelings and circumstances. Accept imperfection in your choices, whether it's illness or job loss.

Facing the uncontrollable is key to progress. With daily practice, you'll feel less powerless over time.

Wanting control over everything is common, but relinquishing it lets us live more freely.

Forgive yourself to make better decisions. Self-acceptance helps us navigate life's challenges.

Recognizing what's beyond our control empowers us. Acceptance allows us to focus on the positive.

Distinguish between regaining control and manipulating outcomes. Take ownership of your actions to avoid self-sabotage.

Mindfulness helps regain control. Awareness prevents manipulation and empowers decision-making.

Accepting solitude fosters self-growth and control.

Surround yourself with positive influences during tough times. Avoid negative influences that exacerbate situations.

Accept uncertainty with optimism to regain control.

Difficult people challenge our sense of control. Learn to understand and accept differences.

This chapter offers techniques to seize control despite circumstances. Building control heightens awareness of personal power.

Adapting to change promotes control. Accept change as an inevitable part of life.

Maintain autonomy by refusing to let others decide for you. Trust yourself and your decisions, prioritizing self-worth.

Evaluate situations honestly to maintain control. Don't let others dictate your choices. Be true to yourself.

Accept mistakes and don't fear making them. People are often willing to help if you ask. Not everyone will agree with you or follow your path. If others don't do things your way, it doesn't mean they're wrong. It's crucial to understand how our actions affect others and avoid hurting them. We all have strengths, but we can't do everything alone. It's okay to ask for help, but sometimes, doing it yourself is better. Others can't change who you are, so don't let them. It's okay if others don't always understand you, even if you're open with them. You'll never know their feelings unless you ask. People can support you even when you don't want them to. It's fine to let others decide sometimes, especially if you're unsure. It can be overwhelming to make all the decisions. You can't dictate how others feel or understand everything they do. Everyone has their perspective, and it's okay if it differs from yours. Here are some ways to exercise control when you're not in charge:

Don't get angry if there's nothing you can do about it. It'll only make things worse.

Plan instead of waiting for things to happen. You can't control others or the future, but you can prepare yourself.

Be ready for unknown problems because life is never easy. Sometimes, you have to accept others' opinions about your plans, but that doesn't mean they know what's best for you. Trust yourself. If you doubt your plans, it might be time to reconsider. You need time for yourself, but helping others isn't wrong if you can manage it. Sometimes, acting out of fear prevents you from moving forward. It's better to try and fail than to remain stuck in fear. You can't please everyone all the time. Focus on what works best for you and make the most of the situation. Be cautious about making plans when others have too much influence. Stay organized but don't stress about things beyond your control. It's okay to be upset, but save your energy for things you can change. Don't let frustrations consume you. Life won't always go as planned, but you can find ways to make it better. Don't give up when things get tough. If others try to hold you back, stand up for yourself. Take control of your life and focus on the positives. Sometimes, you have to accept things won't go your way. But that doesn't mean you can't strive for a better outcome. If everything seems bleak, focus on what you can do to improve. Don't dwell on the negatives. Look for opportunities to enjoy life and pursue your goals. Stay resilient, and things will get better. If life isn't going as expected, reassess your approach. Learn from your mistakes and adjust accordingly. Don't let others discourage you. Keep pushing forward and striving for a better life. When things seem dire, remember you have the power to make a change. Don't let others dictate your happiness. If others try to hinder you, take charge of your life. Don't let anyone stand in the way of your happiness and success.

Gaining Control

Sometimes, things seem tough, and it feels like nothing's going right. But there's more we can do to feel better.

We might find ourselves in situations where life feels challenging. If things aren't getting better, it's up to us to make changes.

If we're struggling, it's time to stop worrying about what others think and focus on making things better for ourselves.

"When life gets tough, we need to figure out how to make it easier, so we can keep doing what we love."

If people are holding us back, it's time to stand up for ourselves and find solutions.

If life feels really hard, we have to decide if it's worth pushing through or finding new ways to enjoy it.

Even when things don't go as planned, there's still hope for a better future if we keep trying.

"The only way forward is to reconnect with ourselves."

We may feel stuck, but we have to keep trying to break free from difficult situations.

If others are blocking our path, we need to take charge of our lives and find our own way forward.

When everything seems wrong, it's time to figure out what we can do to turn things around.

"If life is tough, we have to dig deep and keep going."

We may face obstacles, but with determination, things can get better.

When nothing seems to work, it's a sign to try harder and explore new options.

Life may not be perfect, but we can still find joy and purpose in our journey.

"If life is tough, let's keep pushing forward."

We have to believe in ourselves and keep striving for a better life, even when things are challenging.

"If life isn't what we expected, let's find a new path."

Instead of blaming others, let's focus on what we can do to improve our situation.

"If things aren't working out, let's try something different."

Even when life feels overwhelming, there's always a way to find hope and happiness.

"Let's keep moving forward, even when life gets tough."

In the end, it's up to us to create the life we want, no matter what challenges we face.

Taking Charge of Your Life

Being in control means making sure things go your way. It's about making sure nobody takes away what you want. When you're the one in control, it's not good if you can't do what you want. If you don't want something, others might try to make you do it, causing more problems.

Sometimes, being in control can be tough. You might think that being in control means controlling everything around you, but that's not true. It can lead to more problems.

Being in control can cause problems with other people. To control your own life, you need to learn to let go of things that don't matter.

One important thing is learning to let go and accept things as they are. Holding onto things, like people or situations, can cause issues and take away your power. Being in control of your own life means having power over yourself, not over others.

You can control yourself and your feelings. But you can't control how others feel or what they do to be happy. However, it helps you figure out what you want in life and what doesn't make you happy.

Letting go of things you can't control can help stop anxiety. Doing what you want, even if it means letting go of things you've held onto for a long time, can make you feel better. In life, you'll need to let go of many things to move forward. Whether it's people or situations, letting go can improve your life.

To have control over your life, it's important to let go of things that don't make you feel good about yourself. Even though it can be tough, especially when you feel like you're in charge, it helps to understand what's happening around you. Life becomes easier when you stop worrying about what others are doing or how they feel about you.

It's important to know that nobody, not even someone who seems to control your life, can always give you the results you want. It takes more than just being in control and keeping annoying things away. Feeling like you're always in control and nobody can beat you can lead to anxiety. The problem is, there will always be things you can't control. Relaxing and giving things a chance helps you figure out where your life is headed without stressing over others' actions or feelings.

Feeling in control of everything in your life can cause anxiety. It might feel like nobody else has a say, leaving you isolated. This can cause issues for you and your relationships. If someone close tries to take control and make decisions for you, it can strain your bond. Instead of worrying about how they see you, understand they did it because they care, even if it's not what you wanted.

Not being able to control something can cause anxiety. If there are situations you can't control and you can't change how others think or feel, there's not much you can do.

By learning to let go and stop controlling others, you finally gain control over your life. Letting go empowers you, taking back control from those who seemed to have it. By releasing control, you can stop worrying about things out of your hands and focus on your desires. This kind of anxiety is tough, but not caring about what's beyond your control can boost your self-esteem.

If we keep losing control, others might try to take over. If we're not careful, everything could slip from our grasp, and that won't end well. When you're in control, make sure nobody can take what's yours. Waiting around and hoping things will work out isn't wise. We may need to act if something seems better than what's happening. If you want something badly, chances are others are trying to stop you. It's not good to be in control but living in a situation you don't want.

Life might not seem good when things aren't going as planned, but when they do, it's less likely that other problems will arise.

If we can't stand up for ourselves, it's best to stop dwelling on what others are doing wrong and focus on taking charge of our own situations.

When everything seems chaotic, it's possible that external factors are at play. However, if we desire change, we must take action instead of passively waiting for things to improve.

Wanting something different may require exploring alternative approaches, especially when faced with challenges. But if circumstances are adverse, we might feel compelled to comply with others' expectations.

Relying solely on external influences for solutions may not always yield positive outcomes; sometimes, self-improvement is necessary.

Taking control means actively seeking improvement rather than resigning to a stagnant state.

Life's current state doesn't dictate its future; change is always possible if we're willing to initiate it.

Being proactive in shaping our circumstances ensures a more favorable outcome than merely hoping for the best.

If we're uncertain about the next steps, relying solely on others' decisions isn't prudent; it's essential to take ownership of our choices.

When we exert effort towards our goals, others take notice, increasing the likelihood of achieving desired outcomes.

Recognizing our agency empowers us to pursue a better future, even amidst adversity.

Attempting to control everything can hinder progress; sometimes, relinquishing control is the key to success.

Acknowledging life's uncertainties allows us to adapt and thrive in unpredictable circumstances.

Trusting in life's inherent order doesn't mean resigning to chaos; it means embracing change and seeking opportunities for growth.

Striving for improvement requires action, not mere wishful thinking.

Accepting reality as it is enables us to move forward and effect positive change.

Releasing expectations fosters a deeper understanding of life's complexities.

Resisting the urge to micromanage every aspect of life promotes a more fulfilling existence.

Recognizing our limitations frees us from the burden of trying to control everything.

Experimenting with different approaches is more effective than clinging to rigid expectations.

By exploring various possibilities, we expand our understanding of what's achievable.

To achieve true autonomy, we must release the need to control every outcome.

Instead of fixating on what's wrong, focus on what's within your power to change.

Redefining success means embracing life's uncertainties and adapting accordingly.

Planning for Success

Planning for success means thinking about what might happen and making a plan accordingly. It's not about controlling everything or having fixed ideas about how things should be. A good plan comes from paying attention to what's going on and then planning your actions carefully.

Paying attention makes sense because it helps us understand how things work. You need a plan that works, one that considers the reality of the situation. You can't just wait for good things to happen without putting in any effort. You have to take things one step at a time and be realistic about what you can achieve.

A good plan doesn't ignore reality. It's about taking responsibility for your actions by paying attention to what's happening and thinking about what could go wrong. Planning is a process of observing and exploring, not just imagining things the way you want them to be.

Planning for success means taking action instead of waiting for things to magically work out. It's about managing reality and being realistic about what you can achieve. Success doesn't come from wishing and hoping; it comes from taking action.

It's important to understand that planning takes time. You can't expect everything to change overnight just because you've made a plan. You have to be patient and stick to your plan, even when things don't go as expected.

Stop waiting for things to happen and start taking action. Complaining won't solve anything; you have to take action if you want things to change. Success comes from taking action, not from complaining or wishing things were different.

If you want to succeed, you have to take control of your own life. Don't wait for others to make things happen for you; take charge and make your own success. Stop complaining and start planning for success today.

Life doesn't always go as we hope. Just wishing for good things to happen isn't enough; we need plans and actions to make them a reality. Success doesn't come from waiting for everything to fall into place; it comes from paying attention, making decisions, and taking steps towards our goals.

To start a successful business, you first need a clear idea of what you want to achieve. You can't control everything, and waiting for others to act won't lead to success. If something isn't working, take action to change it. Success requires planning, responsibility, and attention to detail.

False plans won't work because they can't meet expectations. Criticism from others won't help either. It's up to us to take the necessary steps to achieve our goals. No one else can do it for us.

Steven Hicks suggests focusing on what you want in life instead of dwelling on the negative. Control what you can, accept what you can't, and don't expect others to change for you. Success comes from understanding the situation, working on problems, and letting go of perfectionism.

Finally, success won't happen exactly as planned, and that's okay. Let go of expectations, involve others in your plans, and use your time wisely. Change won't happen overnight, but with patience and determination, you can achieve your goals.

In the end, accept that things won't always go your way. People will change if they want to, but you can't force them. Focus on what you can control, take responsibility for your actions, and keep moving forward.

Your Path to Success

Success isn't just reaching a destination; it's a journey full of unexpected twists and turns. Sometimes, you might encounter challenges that seem insurmountable. Life is unpredictable, and we can't control every outcome, no matter how hard we try.

When faced with difficulties, don't give up too easily. There's often a solution waiting to be discovered. Stay flexible and open-minded, because rigidity can hinder progress.

It's never too late to find a solution. Take your time and don't rush into decisions when things seem impossible. Rest is essential for problem-solving, so make sure to give your brain the energy it needs.

If you're unsure how to proceed, focus on the potential benefits of achieving your goal. There's usually more than one way to accomplish something, even if it seems impossible at first.

Even in the most challenging situations, perseverance can lead to success. Keep trying until you've exhausted all options. Enjoy your achievements along the way, as celebrating small victories can motivate you to keep going.

Acceptance is key. Instead of trying to control everything, adapt to the situation and do what you can. Challenges are a natural part of life, but they become problematic when we resist them. Let go of expectations and focus on the present moment.

Trying to change others or expecting them to behave a certain way is futile. People will act according to their own desires and motivations, so it's best not to impose your expectations on them.

To effect change in your life, take control of your own behavior and let go of reliance on others. Focus on your goals and be mindful of your actions.

Avoid distractions and stay committed to your objectives.

Ultimately, success is about navigating life's challenges with resilience and determination. Enjoy the journey, and think that setbacks are opportunities for growth. By staying adaptable and focused, you can overcome any obstacle and achieve your goals.

When others don't get what they want, that's okay! Instead of trying hard to make everything happen just as everyone wants, it's better to let go and move on. You can change your life by dropping all expectations about how things should be and focusing on what can make things turn out fine for everyone. If you pay attention to opportunities and situations that can lead to good outcomes for everyone, you can steer your life in the right direction. Happiness isn't something that always falls into our laps; we need to take charge of our own happiness by finding ways to make things work out the way we want them to, instead of waiting for good things to happen by chance.

It's important to know what you want if you want things to work out well for everyone. Instead of being fixated on how things are supposed to be, it's better to look for ways to change your life for the better. When your mind is set on how things should unfold, you're more likely to make everything turn out well for everyone. You create your own luck.

It's essential to understand that just because you want something doesn't mean you'll get it. Sometimes, we all desire something, but we can't always have it or achieve it. Things don't always go according to plan because there are many possibilities of what might happen, rather than a definite idea of how things should be. If you try to force things to happen your way, they may not work out as they should.

Things don't always unfold as expected because there are many possibilities of what could happen, instead of taking action to ensure a situation turns out in your favor. If people don't get what they want, it's okay! It's better to let go and move forward than to insist on things going their way. If your focus is on how things should pan out, it's easy for a situation to change.

Sometimes, the people we love may not always provide what we need to make everything work out well for everyone involved. Life works out fine for everyone if we focus on opportunities and situations that can lead to positive outcomes for all. Happiness isn't something that's always handed to us; we have to work for it.

Your Strategy for Success

Believing in yourself can change everything in life. It's up to you to make things better or worse based on your desires and how you handle situations. Sometimes, people give up on their dreams because they're not taking action. Complaining won't help if you're not willing to step out of your comfort zone. Trying to force things will only lead to disappointment. With a plan, nothing can stop you from achieving your goals. Improve your life by focusing on the right things and believing in yourself.

You can create the outcome you want in life. Even when facing challenges, there's always a solution if you work hard. Don't wait for things to happen; take action now. Being passive won't lead to any change. Overcome obstacles, and your life will improve because you'll gain valuable experience.

Passion fuels success because passionate people have a vision they can achieve.

It's good to be excited about your goals, but don't be overconfident. Happiness shouldn't depend on others. Think about your accomplishments, even when you're busy. Treat others well, as you want to be treated. Building a strong foundation requires cooperation. Stay calm in frustrating situations. Stay positive and focused to turn negatives into positives. Take things slow if you're unsure where to start. Don't fear the unknown or criticism. The truth always prevails. Don't dwell on negative emotions; look for the bright side. Be accountable for your actions; denying them won't lead to happiness. Find purpose in everything you do. Learn from the past to become better in the future.

What do you want from life? Find inspiration in others' lives. Control your strategies wisely. Take action and focus on what matters. Think like a winner to reach your goals. Success comes from trying and learning. Don't wait for success; take action now.

Battling the Fear of Uncertainty

Preparing for Change When you're making changes, it's smart to get ready for what might come your way. This way, you won't be surprised if things don't turn out as planned, no matter how much you try or want them to. Here are two ways to stay prepared:

a) Predict: Regularly guess how things will turn out in the future, whether good or bad. Sometimes, these guesses may not be entirely accurate.

b) Confidence: Feel confident about what's coming, even before it happens. If you have a sense of what's ahead and believe in it, you're off to a good start.

Why Staying Ready Matters If you're not prepared, you'll never know if there could've been a different outcome. Success often boils down to being ready to seize opportunities and make things happen.

While some fear failure, the truth is, success is within reach for those with the courage to act. The only real failure is giving up without trying at all.

Action Makes the Difference Throughout history, the most significant achievers have one thing in common: they took action. It's those who persevere, even when things seem bleak, that bring their ideas to life. Training yourself to stay prepared and never give up, no matter the obstacles, is key. Though it's not easy, with determination, success becomes possible.

Facing Obstacles Everyone encounters obstacles, but those who face them head-on are more likely to succeed. If you believe in yourself and your potential, nothing can stand in your way. Failure is part of the journey and a chance to learn and grow. Those who doubt their ability to succeed will struggle, while those who believe in themselves will prevail.

Staying Positive Amid Uncertainty Though the future is uncertain, maintaining a positive outlook is crucial. If you're driven by a strong purpose, negativity will hinder your success. Belief in yourself and your goals is essential. Train yourself to face challenges with confidence, regardless of what lies ahead.

Strategies for Success By fighting your weaknesses, you show your determination to overcome the fear of uncertainty. Don't shy away from opportunities to grow. Strive for greatness and remain committed to your goals. Here's what you can do:

Start with a Plan: Define success on your terms and chart a course to achieve it.

Cultivate a Strong Character: Align your decisions with your goals and remain resilient in the face of stress.

Prepare for Adversity: Be ready to adapt if things don't go as planned.

Surround Yourself with Like-minded People: Seek support from those who share your aspirations.

Stay Focused and Positive: Keep negativity at bay and maintain clarity on your objectives.

Persistence Pays Off: Don't give up easily; success often requires time and effort.

Take Ownership: Don't wait for opportunities—create them for yourself.

To wrap up, while fear of the unknown is natural, it shouldn't hold you back. Success is achievable with determination and action. Don't wait for others to make things happen; take charge of your destiny and pursue your dreams relentlessly.

Conquer Your Fears

Everyone feels scared sometimes, but we have to learn how to deal with it. Don't let fear control your life. If you're scared, don't let others tell you what's important. You need to learn how to face your fears and change how you see life.

To be successful, learn from others but never stop doing what you love. You don't need others to like you to be happy. Always know why something is important to you and don't let others control your decisions.

No one is perfect. Don't worry about what others think of you. Believe in yourself, and you can achieve anything you want.

Don't let fear stop you from living your life. Stay positive and believe in yourself. Don't let others control you or bring you down. Focus on yourself and what makes you happy. If someone blames you for something, stand up for yourself and stick to the truth.

Don't let others take advantage of you. Keep your secrets safe and don't let jealousy or fear hold you back. Stay strong and confident in yourself, no matter what happens. Always strive to improve and learn from your mistakes.

Facing your fears head-on can be daunting, but with some practical strategies, you can conquer them. Here are some simple tips to help you fight your fears:

- Write it Down: Grab a piece of paper and jot down your fears. Sometimes, putting them on paper can make them feel less overwhelming.
- Toss it Away: Once you've written down your fears, crumple up the paper and toss it in the bin. It's a symbolic way of letting go of those negative thoughts.

- Make a Why List: List out why you should confront these fears. Seeing the reasons laid out can provide motivation and remind you of the benefits of facing your fears.

- Speak Out Loud: Read aloud what you've written. Hearing your own voice can reinforce your resolve and make your fears feel more manageable.

- Counter Negative Thoughts: Identify the negative aspects of your fears and counter them with positive affirmations about your strengths. Remind yourself of past successes and your ability to overcome challenges.

- Make More Lists: Expand on your initial list of fears. Breaking them down into smaller parts can make them seem less intimidating and easier to tackle one step at a time.

- Mirror Exercise: Spend some time looking at yourself in the mirror. Try to find calmness and reaffirm your identity.

Practice positive self-talk and remind yourself of your worth.

- Change Perspectives: Look at your surroundings from different angles. Sometimes, a fresh perspective can help shift your mindset and make your fears seem less daunting.
- Share a Smile: Smile, even if it's just for yourself. Research has shown that smiling can actually boost your mood and reduce stress, helping you feel more confident and capable.
- Me Time: Take a few minutes each day for yourself. Engage in activities that bring you joy and relaxation, whether it's reading a book, taking a walk, or practicing mindfulness.

- Self-Compassion: Be kind to yourself, regardless of what happens. Treat yourself with the same understanding and compassion you'd offer a friend going through a tough time.

- Visualize Success: Take some time to visualize yourself overcoming your fears and achieving your goals. Imagine how it will feel to conquer your fears and avail new opportunities.

- Seek Support: Don't be afraid to reach out to friends, family, or a therapist for support. Talking about your fears with someone you trust can help alleviate anxiety and provide valuable perspective.

- Take Small Steps: Break down your fears into smaller, manageable steps. Focus on taking one small action at a time, and celebrate each success along the way.

- Challenge Negative Thoughts: Practice challenging negative thoughts and replacing them with more realistic and positive ones. Remind yourself that fear is often based on irrational beliefs and that you have the power to change your mindset.

- Face Your Fears Gradually: Gradually expose yourself to the things that scare you, starting with the least intimidating and working your way up. This can help desensitize you to your fears and build confidence over time.

- Practice Mindfulness: Engage in mindfulness practices such as deep breathing, meditation, or yoga to help calm your mind and reduce anxiety.

- Focus on the Present: Instead of dwelling on past mistakes or worrying about the future, focus on the present moment. Practice being mindful and fully engaged in whatever you're doing right now.

- Celebrate Your Progress: Acknowledge and celebrate your progress, no matter how small. Give yourself credit for facing your fears and taking steps towards personal growth and development.

- Believe in Yourself: Above all, believe in yourself and your ability to overcome obstacles. Trust that you have the strength, resilience, and courage to face your fears and create the life you desire.

How To Overcome Fear

Fear stops us from trying new things and can hold us back from making the choices we want in our lives. If we don't know how to face our fears, we will never achieve the goals we set for ourselves. Fear makes us feel nervous and uncomfortable, but learning to overcome it will allow us to do everything we've ever wanted. Fear makes us live in the past and prevents us from focusing on the future. If we face our fears instead of running away, nothing can stop us from achieving our dreams. Fear often makes us take the easy way out and stops us from trying new things, but if we use fear to our advantage, we can achieve greatness. It keeps us from living a happy life and achieving our goals.

Fear controls our lives and holds us back from good things, but facing it directly can make everything fall into place. If you're feeling nervous or uneasy, tell yourself it's normal and nothing to be afraid of. Sometimes fear can be good because it shows us what we're doing wrong and helps us understand why we shouldn't keep doing the same things. Fear can take so much away if we let it control us, but facing our fears can make everything better.

Here are some steps to control and overcome fear:

- Make a plan for how you want to overcome your fear.
- Go for it and learn from your mistakes.
- Trust yourself and your ability to make changes.
- Once you overcome fear, focus on living your dreams.

Fear makes us think we can't do what we want in life, but facing our fears will make everything better. Accept that there will be things we're afraid of, but taking steps in the right direction and facing our fears will make it easier to overcome them.

Overcoming fear can make a big difference in your everyday life.

Face your fears instead of letting them control you because if fear controls you, nothing will be good until you learn to deal with it. When you overcome fear, the world will look better to you and keep getting better.

To be successful and accomplish your goals, you have to conquer your fears. Facing our fears teaches us how to overcome them instead of letting them control us and cause stress. It helps us understand what's wrong in our lives so we can fix it and prevent the same thing from happening again. If we don't, everything will go downhill for us.

The following additional tips will greatly help you overcome fear:

- Understand that fear is a normal human emotion. Everyone feels it, but the key to success is not letting it control your life. Those who do not overcome fear often live unhappily and never reach their full potential.

- Think positively and you can overcome anything you fear.
- Keep moving forward because fear will never disappear unless you decide to confront it. If you keep moving, fear will eventually leave because it isn't strong enough to stop you.
- Ensure that your fear is based on reality before letting it control your life. Worrying about something that will never happen is a waste of time and energy.
- Consider how great your life will be after you overcome the fear holding you back.
- Fear is just an emotion that warns you, but if you let it control you, it will prevent you from achieving your goals.
- Surround yourself with people who motivate you and eliminate those who bring negativity into your life. Focus on positivity and good feelings.

- When faced with two choices, always choose the one that brings positive feelings into your life.
- Take action to reach your full potential. Waiting for things to happen on their own will not lead to success.
- Don't be afraid to talk about your feelings. Facing them head-on will help you get rid of them for good.
- Never give up because of something scary. Overcoming fear is essential to achieving your dreams and living a happy life.
- Use your fears to improve your life. Turn what scares you into a positive force.
- Focus on making your life better instead of worrying about failure. Worrying holds you back from achieving your dreams and important life goals.
- Try to understand things from other people's perspectives. Everyone has fears, and dealing with them positively can improve your life.

- Be confident in yourself and your feelings. Confidence helps you live outside of fear.
- Recognize that fear is a part of life. Overcoming it is the only way to improve your life. Understanding your fears is better than ignoring them.
- Accept that bad things happen. Trying to avoid them only keeps you in a negative cycle. Deal with problems head-on to avoid getting stuck.
- If you don't know how to handle your fear, don't let it stop you from doing what you need to do.
- Open up about your fears or face them directly to overcome them. This ensures that fear won't control you.
- Address issues right away instead of postponing them. Delaying problems only makes them worse over time.

Conclusion

As we conclude, it's crucial to recognize that our self-esteem shapes who we are more than other people's opinions. To illustrate, consider a job interview scenario. In interviews, negative feedback from previous employers or past experiences might arise, affecting our confidence. However, these external opinions should not deter us from pursuing our goals. Despite potential setbacks, it's essential to prioritize our own beliefs and choices.

It's paramount never to let fear obstruct our path to success. If something doesn't serve us positively, it's best avoided. Giving too much weight to others' opinions can lead to undue influence and complications in our lives.

Avoid allowing external influences to control your actions. Doing so can lead to significant long-term challenges. Remember, if fear guides your decisions, it could lead to unfavorable outcomes.

Instead, focus on yourself and your well-being. When you prioritize self-care and personal growth, you naturally inspire those around you. It's essential to understand others' perspectives while staying true to yourself. Balancing strength and vulnerability makes us stronger individuals.

There are several reasons to avoid being overly concerned with others' opinions:

Taking time to understand different viewpoints enriches our lives.

Living authentically is essential, as letting others dictate our lives has negative consequences.

Worrying about others' thoughts only hampers our progress.

Being genuine and true to oneself is paramount, regardless of external opinions.

It's crucial not to let fear hinder your journey towards success:

Disregarding others' opinions is crucial, especially if they don't align with your values.

Positive thinking outweighs negative influences.

Allowing others to control your life leads to long-term issues.

Focusing on your path rather than external judgments is key.

If someone disapproves of you or your choices, it's best to ignore their input. Remember, you have control over your thoughts, feelings, and actions, regardless of external opinions.

Ultimately, your happiness and well-being depend on how you handle situations emotionally. While others may have opinions, allowing them to dictate your life leads to dissatisfaction. It's essential to assert control over your life decisions, relationships, and activities.

Fear of others' opinions should not dictate your actions. Criticism is inevitable on the path to success. However, your happiness and success are determined by your emotional resilience and self-assurance. Understanding others' perspectives while asserting your own autonomy is crucial for personal growth and fulfillment.

Join My Community

A. Please scan the books series

   "Life Mastery".

B. Please scan the book series,

   "The Art of Living"

www.ingramcontent.com/pod-product-compliance
Lightning Source LLC
Chambersburg PA
CBHW072017230526
45479CB00008B/212